Beautiful Sayings

Beatitudes of Grace

Greg Albrecht

Published by Plain Truth Ministries
Pasadena, CA I www.ptm.org

Scripture: Unless noted otherwise, scriptures are quoted from the *Holy Bible, NIV.* © International Bible Society. UBP of Zondervan.

Emphases: All emphases throughout this book are the author's, including those in Scripture texts and cited material, unless otherwise indicated.

Printed in Canada by Friesens Corp.
Altona, Manitoba, Canada

ISBN: 978-1-889973-39-5

Library of Congress Control Number:
Albrecht, Greg, 1947 –
Beautiful Sayings: Beatitudes of Grace /
Greg Albrecht
1. Religion – Christianity – Beatitudes

Cover Design and Layout: Brad Jersak

CWRpress
An imprint of Plain Truth Ministries

CWR Press is pleased to publish
this special limited edition of
Beautiful Sayings: Beatitudes of Grace

Contents

Preface

Over the centuries many casual Bible readers have mistakenly assumed the world in which Jesus lived, taught and served was peaceful – almost idyllic. Far from a utopia or nirvana-like place of physical prosperity and spiritual harmony, the land in which he was born and was crucified was a spiritual and physical battleground. Palestine was occupied by the harsh and brutal methods of the Roman military. It was a place of horrific oppression, rampant disease and tyrannical taxation.

All families could hope for was to stay safe and alive. "Getting ahead" somewhat like North American dreams in the 20th and 21st centuries was not on the agenda. People did not enjoy sitting down with friends and neighbors, having coffee and quietly reading their Study Bibles. Day to day life was filled with tension, fear and hysteria.

Animosity and dog-eat-dog fighting characterized both the secular and the religious world. Religion was filled with one-upmanship, polarized partisan squabbles, pride, self-righteousness, and bitter condemnation. Compassion and care were rare in a religious world far more intent on religious performance.

During 2020 the COVID pandemic introduced us all to an unseen, deadly enemy that radically changed a "normal" and predictable world, turning it upside down. Perhaps this pandemic might give us a better insight into the fragile life we all actually lead, and the eternal values that transcend all human life and cultures. These are stormy times in which we now live.

Jesus' first century world did not, of course, socially distance itself or wear masks to help prevent the spread of physical and/or spiritual toxins, yet Jesus was a calming presence in the midst of that crowded, angry and hostile world. He still is. When we see Jesus through this lens, the Beautiful Sayings of his Beatitudes offer staggering insights into God's amazing grace and peace.

Jesus was the love of God in the midst of corruption, muck and mire. He revealed the love of the Father in the midst of violence and suffering. Jesus was then and remains now an oasis of rest and peace in the middle of raging storms. Jesus' transcendent message cuts through the noise all around us.

In both his behavior and his teachings Jesus reached out to the downtrodden, offering healing and grace to all those in bondage. He pierced through the crippling aggression of the rich and the slavery of religious power brokers. Jesus flipped the script of what is fair and just, upending traditional ethical assumptions and religious traditions. The Beatitudes then seemed so illogical and counter-intuitive and they still do. Jesus' teaching reveals the eternal and divine value of vulnerability in the face of danger and gentleness in the midst of hatred.

Now when Jesus saw the crowds, he went up on a mountainside and sat down. His disciples came to him, and he began to teach them. He said:

Blessed are the poor in spirit, for theirs is the kingdom of heaven.

Blessed are those who mourn, for they will be comforted.

Blessed are the meek, for they will inherit the earth.

Blessed are those who hunger and thirst for righteousness, for they will be filled.

Blessed are the merciful, for they will be shown mercy.

Blessed are the pure in heart, for they will see God.

Blessed are the peacemakers, for they will be called children of God.

Blessed are those who are persecuted because of righteousness, for theirs is the kingdom of heaven.

Blessed are you when people insult you, persecute you and falsely say all kinds of evil against you because of me. Rejoice and be glad, because great is your reward in heaven, for in the same way they persecuted the prophets who were before you.
– Matthew 5:1-12

These eight Beatitudes are the introduction to what has come to be called the Sermon on the Mount, the summary teachings recorded by Matthew in chapters five, six and seven. At the conclusion of the three chapters Matthew observes: *When Jesus had finished saying these things, the crowds were amazed at his teaching, because he taught as one who had authority, and not as their teachers of the law* – Matthew 7:28-29. **Jesus was and is a different kind of preacher and teacher.**

Religious teachers at that time depended heavily on the traditional regulations and requirements of those who had gone before them. The story of Christ-less religion is revealed in its history – much like archaeology, religion has laid down layers and levels of generational strata one after another, each built and dependent upon the past. Christ-less religion is a house of cards because it's all predicated upon previous generations, the mistakes of which, Jesus says, were built on sand, rather than the rock of his teachings. The foundational presuppositions of religion and those who articulated it have been reverentially believed and accepted without question. Not much has changed over the past two thousand years, has it?

The teaching and preaching of Jesus, like an earthquake,

exposed and laid bare massive fissures and faults in the religion of his day and the assumptions upon which it had been built. The preaching and teaching of Jesus was entirely different than what that culture was used to hearing from their religious leaders. ***Here was an altogether different kind of preacher*** whose authority did not rest upon dead theologians. The crowds were astonished.

Immediately following the eight Beatitudes, Jesus contrasted his teaching with the "religious party line" that people expected to hear. Matthew provides six units of teaching (Matthew 5:21-48) in which Jesus' teaching differs with the ethical demands of religion. Some call these six paradigms of Jesus' teaching ***antithetical statements*** because Jesus begins each example by reiterating a formulaic saying, that goes something like, *"You have heard that thus and such has been said, but I say unto you"* (see Matthew 5:21, 27, 31, 33, 38 and 43).

There is no doubt that Jesus was and is an altogether different kind of preacher and teacher!

What the Sermon on the Mount Does

In his book *A More Christlike Way*, published by CWRpress in 2019, my friend Brad Jersak discusses the Beatitudes and the Sermon on the Mount. Dr. Jersak notes that the Sermon on the Mount is the core of Jesus' teachings, and as Jesus' interpretation of the law and the prophets it is the pinnacle of the Christlike Way. He speaks of it as "a *Way*. A specific, practical, commanded *Way* to live and Way to life. It is the *Jesus* Way" (pg. 148).

Answering the question about what the Sermon on the Mount does, Dr. Jersak inspires us with these words:

"I can tell you what it does. It pushes my buttons! If you are willing to let Christ sow these words into your heart – if you really hear them and put them into practice – this message will plow the soil of your heart and then plant new seeds of life.

Christ's words will empty you and then they will fill you.

They will deconstruct and reconstruct you – they will renovate, restore and refurbish you.

They will purge you of all the dross that is "not of love's kind," purifying the gold of your true self. They will cleanse the diamond of your heart of the tarnish so that every facet shines with the light of Christ.

If we'll surrender to these words of Jesus, they will not return void. They will accomplish what they purposed to do from the start.

These words of Christ are simple but not easy. Love your enemies, forgive your debtors, trust Abba daily – such words are a litmus test of the heart. They are a diagnostic tool that roots out every hint of rebellion and toxic religion. These words of Christ are intended to lay out your heart, to tenderize it, to salt and season it, and throw it on the barbecue. To be a living sacrifice (a la Rom. 12:1) is *not* about punishment. It's about becoming the aroma of *Grace* that smells like the good news of Jesus's love (pg. 156).

What does the Sermon on the Mount do?

It saves me from believing that I am the center of the universe. It assures me that the world does not revolve and orbit around me.

It saves me from believing I am God or that I need to be God. It saves me from having to manage everyone else's joy, sorrows and choices.

It exposes my inability to manage others.

It exposes my inability to manage myself.

It exposes my inability to manage God.

It IS step one of my recovery.

For me, it began when Beatitude #1 showed me the painful truth that I really do still think I am Lord and that everyone and everything, even God, should be my servant. It walked me through the narrow door to the Kingdom where Jesus is Lord and it is *not* about *I, me,* or *mine* or about *my* will and *my* freedom and *my* rights. I thought *my* freedom was the highest moral imperative. The Sermon says Christ's love of God, neighbor, stranger and enemy is our guiding star.

I thought, like Alice in Wonderland, 'I MAKE the path.'

Christ says, 'I AM the path.'

I thought, 'I am free. I shape my destiny.'

Christ said, 'Follow me. Listen to my words. Do what I say. Then you'll be free.'

But I so much wanted to be god. To be independent, self-sufficient, in control. The *Grace* of the Sermon exposed that in me. And then it stripped it from me and starved it out of me (as much as I let it, in fits and starts, a day at a time). And then it re-clothed me. And re-fed me. Or at least it will" (pgs. 158-159).

The Preacher Who
Delivered the Sermon

Jesus Christ was a ***different kind of preacher and teacher.*** He still is! His message and teachings were revolutionary and his persona and manner of relating to others was radically at odds with the status quo roles exemplified by religious professionals. He did not expect or require others to serve him or bow before him.

He washed his disciple's feet, not the other way around (John 13:1-12). The entire life of Jesus on this earth was a life of foot-washing – he never stopped washing the feet of those he served. He never stopped serving and giving.

He was a different kind of a preacher and teacher because he did not expect people to come to him, but rather he went to them. The world then, as the world now, desperately needed to know and hear and see the love, mercy and grace of God, so his mission was devoted to being with people where they were.

In keeping with his ministry as God coming down into this world, incarnated in the man Jesus, he revealed the love of God by traveling and meeting people where they worked and lived, in the places of their needs, hurts and pains.

He was a different kind of preacher and teacher because he always – always – cared and helped and put others ahead of his own interests, needs and desires. Luke records the parable of Jesus about a good Samaritan (Luke 10:25-37).

Jesus was the Good Samaritan who stopped the man who had been so badly beaten he was left for dead, while two religious professionals, a priest and a Levite, *passed by on the other side* (Luke 10:31-32). There were no "other sides" for Jesus – he was on the side of everyone to whom he ministered, served and preached.

He was a different kind of preacher and teacher because the least and the lost and the last were always a priority for him. His ministry and his teachings were lived out by him in his exceptional love for the poor, the marginalized, the abused, the diseased, the un-forgiven, the forgotten and the fatherless. He valued devalued women and loved unloved children.

He was a different kind of preacher and teacher because he did not depend on religious institutions to instruct him about his ministry. At first the religious professionals discredited him because he was not a product of their educational systems, and then later they came to hate and despise him.

They called him a rabble rouser and a troublemaker. The religious authorities considered him a threat, and discredited him in any way they could. They called him a bastard son of a young girl who became pregnant before marriage.

The Jesus Way

He walked a different walk and lived a different life than religious professionals, then or since. He never wrote a book. He never owned a home. He never got married and never had a family. He never went to college. His only credentials to say and do what he did rested on his claim to be God in the flesh.

He didn't win any awards and trophies because he taught us to turn the other cheek. He didn't win the first century equivalent of the Nobel Peace Prize even though he taught his followers and students to love their enemies. He was not praised and lauded because he was a good man and because he loved others. His self-sacrificial love was not recognized or appreciated. He was not thanked and praised because he put the needs of others ahead of his own.

As we read between the lines of the Four Gospels it seems clear that everyone, apart from the religious community, found Jesus to be an enjoyable person to be around. It seems they walked from miles around to listen to him. It didn't matter who they were – monied or impoverished, entitled or living on the street, healthy or diseased ... they found him fascinating, refreshing and almost irresistible.

What did his virtues and service and love earn him, in the kingdoms of this world? The kingdom of Rome, spurred on by the kingdom of the majority religion of his culture, joined forces to get rid of him – through torture, humiliation and publicly shaming him before they finished him off (or so they thought) by mercilessly crucifying him. He responded by accepting and receiving their (and our own) vengeance and hostility. He soaked it in. He absorbed and assimilated all human hostility and hatred ... and he forgave it.

For Jesus the end of violence is not more violence. The end of violence is love.

Jesus did not demand that we obey him. He did not threaten those who refused and rejected him. He did not promise those who obeyed his teachings with their best life now. Instead, he invited all who would follow him to pick up their own cross and follow in his footsteps.

Jesus didn't peddle a program that promised to improve the lives of his followers. He promised instead a new life for those who died to their own lives, surrendering their lives to his and in turn serving others in his name.

Jesus did not threaten, intimidate or shame people into changing their behavior so that it lined up with his own.

Jesus came to lift us out of shame and guilt and fear – not to add to our enormous burdens of self-loathing. He didn't come to start a new religion or slightly modify and upgrade one that was already in place.

He didn't offer a way in which his followers could live more moral lives by virtue of the character they would build if they faithfully obeyed all the steps he advocated. He didn't tell his followers to prove their worth to him by climbing the highest mountain and fording every stream, because the mountains are higher than our abilities to climb and the rivers deeper and more deadly than our abilities to swim.

Jesus invited us to yield to his overtures of love, and admit to our own vulnerabilities and inabilities. Jesus promised to live his life within us as we yield to him. The Beatitudes are his promises for those who follow him.

Beautiful Sayings

The eight Beatitudes that introduce the three-chapter Sermon on the Mount in Matthew are a condensation and summary of the heart and core of Jesus' teachings – the bedrock of the gospel (good news) of Jesus Christ. The Beatitudes are beautiful sayings because they describe the life of a Christ-follower – they are beautiful because they are the attributes that Jesus produces in the lives of those who follow him.

The Beatitudes are *descriptive* of what Jesus does and will do in the lives of his followers – *they are not prescriptions* or lesson plans for those who will become blessed because of their own blood, sweat and tears.

For some reason, the most vocal Christians among us never mention the Beatitudes (Matthew 5). But, often with tears in their eyes, they nevertheless demand that the Ten Commandments be posted in public buildings. And, of course, that's Moses, not Jesus. I haven't heard one of them demand that the Sermon on the Mount, the Beatitudes, be posted anywhere. "Blessed are the merciful" in a courtroom? "Blessed are the peacemakers" in the Pentagon? Give me a break.

– Kurt Vonnegut, *A Man Without a Country*

The three chapters in Matthew that have come to be called The Sermon on the Mount (Matthew 5-7) are damning evidence that much of what passes for Christianity in our world is just another religion filled with rules, rituals, routines and regulations. Christ-less religion in our world is predicated on coercion and enforcement, resulting in suppression and oppression – the polar opposite of the non-violence taught by Jesus in the Sermon on the Mount.

The prescriptions and pills insisted on by Christendom at large are in diametric contrast with this harmonious masterpiece – called a sermon, but no doubt a compilation of teachings Jesus often reiterated.

In the first chapter of the Sermon as recorded by Matthew, Jesus teaches that the law is impossible to fulfill. Many completely miss this vital perspective. They interpret Jesus as insisting on an even more strict observance of the law for his followers than had been the case in the old covenant. But what Jesus is saying is that since no one can be perfect by observing the law, there is a better way, and that way is his gospel.

Matthew's version of the Sermon on the Mount (Luke 6:17-49 records an abbreviated version) amounts to 111 verses within three chapters (Matthew 5-7). However, one needs no more evidence that much of contemporary Christendom does not speak for Jesus than these eight Beatitudes summarized in the 12 introductory verses.

So again – to reiterate – the first 12 verses of what has come to be known as the Sermon on the Mount are called the Beatitudes – these eight Beatitudes, encapsulated within a foundational tithe of the entire Sermon, provide a startling contrast between Christ and Christendom.

The Beatitudes are counter-cultural to an entrenched Christian culture that since the days of Constantine has been hell bent on "evangelizing" through enforced conformity and ultimately subjugation rather than proclaiming the grace of God and the transformation he freely gives, through Christ, *the hope of glory* (Colossians 1:27).

In a world dominated then and now by the lethal, oppressive combination of warfare and violence on the one hand with the tyranny of fear-based religion on the other, the Beatitudes are the revolutionary manifesto of the kingdom of heaven.

The Beatitudes are antithetical to the dogmas and rituals and endless lists of Christ-less religion because they insist that spiritual transformation by God's grace is a gift, received within and then, after a miraculous internal change of heart, expressed externally, by the dynamic, empowering inner life of our risen Lord. *In the Beatitudes Jesus is not prescribing a list of entrance requirements for the kingdom of heaven.*

Religion (even when it vainly appropriates the name of Christ) and government are the two heads of the beast that oppresses all humanity, utilizing its weapons of laws, authority, conformity, intimidation, humiliation, superstition and fear. Religion and government crucified Jesus then and they continue to crucify his teachings now.

In Matthew's version of the Sermon, the Beatitudes of Jesus are taught as eight pronouncements or definitions of a supernatural experience, blessings of contentedness and peace, a peace (the *shalom)* of God, given by him rather than achieved or earned by humanity.

But, the Beatitudes, along with the longer Sermon they introduce, are interpreted by religion at large to be the moral teachings of Jesus. It's the only possible interpretation by religious ideologies based on laws and rules. When understood merely as the moral teachings of an itinerant Jewish prophet, invariably the Beatitudes are taught and interpreted in such a way that humans bear the responsibility for producing these divine attitudes.

Properly understood these eight qualities/traits/attributes are not intended as lofty plateaus to which dedicated Christians will ascend, after continual browbeating, abstinence, denial and effort. These eight qualities/traits/attributes are gifts produced by the inner presence of the life of Jesus, the "being" rather than "doing" that results from his life lived within those who follow him. We might call them **Be-attitudes**.

• These eight *Be-attitudes* are foreign attitudes to human experience apart from God.

• These eight *Be-attitudes* are ways of being impossible to gain or produce by human effort alone.

• These eight *Be-attitudes* are ways of living produced by God in us – they are his handiwork – not our own.

• These eight *Be-attitudes* are the very mind of Jesus Christ, who lives his risen life in Christ-followers.

• These eight *Be-attitudes* are therefore gifts of God's grace rather than being produced by human religious effort and performance.

• These **eight spiritual blessings**, these **eight contented and peaceful ways of living** are **gifts of God's grace** – they describe what life in Christ looks like. A Christ-follower who accepts and trusts Jesus alone, who yields to God's grace, can expect these to be evidenced in their life as they mature in him.

"If we didn't already know but were asked to guess the kind of people Jesus would pick out for special commendation, we might be tempted to guess one sort or another of spiritual hero – men and women of impeccable credentials morally, spiritually, humanly, and every which way. If so, we would be wrong... They're not what you'd call a high-class crowd – peasants and fisherfolk for the most part, on the shabby side, not all that bright. It doesn't look like there's a hero among them..."

– Frederick Buechner, *Whistling in the Dark*, 19-20.

A Way of Life

The Greek word *makarios* describes how a person *feels* when they are happy and contented. In the first of these eight blessings, Jesus said that the poor in spirit are *makarios* - they are happy.

But it seems those who translated *makarios* into English may have decided it would sound trite to say that someone who is poor in spirit is happy. So instead they used the word "blessed."

Throughout the world of Christendom everyone wants to be "blessed." Those who read and study the Bible want to be blessed, so they understand the implication behind the first Beatitude something like this: "*If* you are poor in spirit, *then* God will bless you." But Jesus didn't say that. Taking the entire gospel into consideration and context, Jesus was saying something like this: "Those who live in me, and I in them, will be happy and content, and they will be poor in spirit."

Jesus did not say we would *have* poverty of spirit, but that we would *be* poor in spirit. The Beatitudes are what we are, in Christ, by God's grace. The Beatitudes are a state of being, a way of life. The Beatitudes are *the Jesus Way*. The Beatitudes are not characteristics or attributes that we gain and thus characteristics we have and possess through our efforts.

Many read the Beatitudes as if Jesus is giving instructions about eight characteristics that humans must somehow manufacture and produce using their own willpower.

But Jesus is not giving a list of self-help rules for better living. Jesus is not giving prescriptions for happy living, rather he is providing descriptions of the blessings given by the *shalom* (peace) of God. The shalom of God is his peace he gives us when we rest in Jesus and when Jesus lives within us, as the King of the kingdom of heaven.

These eight blessings describe and illustrate the kind of life and well-being that God gives to those who accept his gracious invitation. These are eight blessings *from* God. These eight blessings are *gifts of God's grace*. These eight blessings are *the fruit of God's Spirit*, eight attributes that are *produced by God within us*.

There are no imperatives in this listing of eight blessings that Jesus gives. Everything that Jesus describes is in the indicative mood. Jesus is describing the kingdom of heaven, now, and in the future.

The Beatitudes are NOT
Self-Help Rules

As we study the Beatitudes, it seems Jesus begins this list of eight blessings with perhaps the most foundational of Christ-centered attitudes – the most fundamental of all of the gifts of God's grace, and then moves progressively to blessings that build on each other. So, if this assumption is correct, then each of these blessings systematically leads to the next one, in order as Jesus teaches them.

We might perceive these eight blessings as divided in two: the first four seem to focus on our relationship with God while the remaining four are more concerned with our relationship to our fellow humans.

Another feature or theme we will note as we study these eight blessings, these eight *Be-attitudes* (attitudes and blessings that begin to grow and increase in our lives as we mature in Christ) are actually the polar opposite of the values humans normally expect and desire.

These eight Beatitudes are perhaps the most compact and comprehensive definition of the kingdom of heaven, or as Scripture also calls it, the kingdom of God. They are not self-help rules, but rather, the ever-maturing mind of Christ. They are blessings within those who follow him and in whom he lives his risen life.

In these eight blessings Jesus seems to deliberately contrast an attribute, or state of mind or state of living considered to be exalted and supreme in the kingdoms of this world, including the kingdom of religion, and reverses it – he turns the social order and the expected status quo upside down. These eight blessed ways of living and being are a condensed and compact description of *the Jesus Way*.

The Beatitudes
of Christendom

According to the message you will hear in many churches the Beatitudes are taught more like this:

• *Blessed are those who are well off and in need of nothing, they have it all.*

• *Blessed are those who are comfortable, because they can avoid pain and heartache.*

• *Blessed are those who are not troubled with injustices experienced by others, or by the sufferings of those around them. Those who are blessed shut their eyes and ears to the cries of others, and they are not troubled by them.*

• *Blessed are those who can push others around and*

take advantage of them, for they are able to do unto others before others do unto them. Rejoice and be exceedingly glad. Life doesn't get any better than this!

The kingdom of heaven reverses what are commonly assumed as optimal, happy and perfect conditions. The poor in spirit are welcomed into the kingdom of heaven, the spiritually hungry are fed, those who mourn are comforted, those who weep rejoice and those who are powerless become powerful.

While we are limiting our focus to the eight Beatitudes, one more comment about the larger Sermon on the Mount. It was a sermon on a mountain, and there is no doubt that this title was meant by Matthew to contrast the old covenant law, which was given on another mountain (Mt. Sinai) with this clear articulation of the new covenant.

The old covenant law was given on a mountain which the Israelites were forbidden to touch, on the pain of death. The mountain was filled with earthquakes and thunder, and the law was given in an atmosphere of fear. ***Do this or else***.

But there are no threats or terror contained in the Sermon on the Mount. The foundational principles of the new covenant, the gifts of God's grace, are proclaimed by Jesus. The Beatitudes are promises of the blessings, joy and inner peace he will produce in the lives of those who follow him.

All of these eight Beatitudes are ***descriptive rather than prescriptive***. They describe what a citizen of the kingdom of heaven looks like because of the gifts of God, rather than what a citizen looks like because of their hard work which produced these qualities.

- The Beatitudes reveal what a citizen of the kingdom looks like, what a child of God looks like, once he or she has yielded their life, like a lump of clay, to the Master Potter, who forms and shapes that life into a new creation for his glory. Children of God look like Jesus, God in the flesh, not Christ-less religion.

- The Beatitudes are not Jesus saying, "Live like this and I will then be pleased to call you one of my disciples."

- The Beatitudes are a portrait drawn by Jesus of the life of one who accepts his grace. The Beatitudes are a spiritual mirror that reflects the love and grace of God as it grows and matures in the life of those who follow Jesus Christ.

The First Beatitude

Blessed are the poor in spirit,
for theirs is the kingdom of heaven.
– Matthew 5:3

The poor in spirit are *makarios*: the blessed and happy peaceful state of one on whom God confers his favor. While some suggest *makarios* should be translated as *happy*, modern usage has devalued "happy" so that it falls far short of the blessed peace (Hebrew *shalom*) experienced by the poor in spirit.

Because Jesus lives within them the poor in spirit do not think *more highly than they ought* (Romans 12:3) of themselves. Christ-followers are not overly impressed with human strength and self-sufficiency. Those who are, by God's grace, poor in spirit, recognize their weaknesses and reflect Christ-centered humility that opposes spiritual arrogance and pride.

Physical impoverishment is not one and the same as being poor in spirit. Poverty can be a curse that arises from many un-Christlike activities and behaviors, and as such Jesus is not praising physical impoverishment. The poverty of spirit Jesus speaks about is the willingness to surrender all earthly security while joyfully embracing the heavenly kingdom.

Later in the Sermon on the Mount, Jesus says, *For where your treasure is, there will your heart be also* – Matthew 6:21. The beautiful saying about the poor in spirit explains they are given the kingdom of heaven.

When our treasure is in heaven, when our treasure is Christ-centered, then we are not obsessed with the trinkets of desire-based consumerism and materialism. The focus of the hearts of those who are poor in spirit transcends here-today-and-gone-tomorrow earthly goods and comforts in favor of the eternal riches of God's grace.

Human beings naturally want to be comfortable and secure. We are easily distracted and deceived by stuff which we come to think of as bringing us happiness. But Jesus counters that notion by saying spiritual peace flows out of the divine gift of being poor in spirit.

The poor in spirit are not motivated by fear, shame and guilt in such a way that they assume doing all of the right religious things – for example, "going" to church (thinking of the body of Christ primarily as *a place we go* rather than *who and what we are,* by God's grace) will bring them spiritual riches. Paying tithes or offerings, praying regularly, getting involved in church programs and outreaches, making sure you do all of the right things in the right way and at the right places does not equate to being poor in spirit.

It is, of course, possible to be involved in beneficial projects and virtuous deeds and be poor in spirit, but anything one might perform or produce, even in the name of God, does not mean that the direct result (*ipso facto*) of such work will result in one being poor in spirit.

God does not need nor is he obligated by our religious performances. Sadly, it's virtually inevitable that the production of religious stuff makes people feel that God is obligated to them. Many religious people feel that God must reward their religious trophies, blue ribbons, diplomas, certificates and commendations. And that attitude leads to pride, the antithesis of the attitude of Jesus, which is humility. The humility of Jesus is the impoverishment of the human spirit.

The Second Beatitude

Blessed are those who mourn, for they shall be comforted.
– Matthew 5:4

Assuming these eight blessings to be cumulative, let's consider how *blessed are those who mourn* progressively builds on *blessed are the poor in spirit*. Christ-followers rest in him, trusting him and they are divinely empowered to recognize their spiritual poverty. The recognition of absolute need of God is an important building block of one's relationship with God.

In many of his epistles Paul explained that we cannot live in Christ unless and until we die to Christ, so that we may live in him. So again, assuming that *blessed are those who mourn* builds upon *blessed are the poor in spirit* we can see that when God leads us to see and believe how dependent we are in him, then we mourn.

Christ in us causes and gives rise to our mourning as we realize how proud and presumptuous we once were (when we were apart from him) to assume that God would be obligated to bless us because of what we considered to be righteous deeds that we performed.

When we are poor in spirit, we recognize our absolute need of God, and that leads us to sorrow and grieve. We are distressed and regret the kind of prideful people we used to be and the arrogance and independence from God that so described our past lives.

We mourn, wondering why and how we could have ever been so impressed with ourselves. The mourning Jesus is talking about is one of the strongest words for "mourn" used in the Bible, speaking of the emotions felt when one loses a loved one. Spiritually, we mourn the self-absorbed, religious life we once led and how empty and vain it was and give thanks for God's comfort as he gives us new life in Christ.

Within contemporary Christendom, feel good/think-and-grow-rich/health-and-wealth religion is relentlessly expounded in huge mega-churches, with multiple thousands seemingly hanging on every word of someone who is adorned in polished finery. They sport expensive suits and fancy watches. Looking at the external veneer of such preachers and teachers, one can't imagine such a person ever having a problem.

These salesmen of what is called ***the prosperity gospel*** seem to have God in their hip pocket. They urge us to claim blessings from God, to demand them and therefore to "have our best life now" but this Beatitude, this blessing from God about mourning, points us in the opposite direction.

This blessing about mourning leads us into the direction of suffering. All who live in Christ will suffer, all who are Christ-followers will, by definition, pick up their cross and follow him.

The Greek root for this word "comforted" has as much, or perhaps more, to do with being strengthened and helped rather than being consoled and relieved of afflictions and encumbrances. Christ in us will help us to 1) recognize our need of God, 2) to be sorrowful and repent of our pride and self-centeredness, and comfort (strengthen and encourage) us to carry our respective crosses.

The Third Beatitude

Blessed are the meek, for they will inherit the earth.
– Matthew 5:5

The person who is blessed and given the gift of meekness is someone who has surrendered his or her own desires and goals so that they are willing to live by God's grace, rather than their own self-serving self-sufficiency.

Meekness, a gift of God, is a submissive and trusting attitude toward God. Those who are blessed and given the gift of meekness trust in God to provide for them rather than presuming their own efforts to be the final determining factor as to the success or failure of their life. The person who is blessed and given the gift of meekness is anything but weak; in God's eyes he or she is truly strong in the Lord.

It is true that the meekness of Jesus is often understood by the kingdoms of this world as weakness, but that's only true because the kingdoms of this world value brute strength, intimidation and the power of oppression.

This gift of meekness is the humility of Jesus Christ, not borne out of weakness, but borne out of the strength of Jesus. Jesus alone, the Creator of the entire universe, Lord of all, can provide this meekness.

The meek are meek because Jesus imparts his own humility and patience to them – he lives out his own meekness as he lives his risen life within them. Remember the meekness of Jesus:

• He was the God of Creation, yet he was gentle and kind, patient and compassionate with his creation.

• He embodied humility, simplicity and service.

• He who was eternally rich came out of the riches of heaven so that we, spiritually poor, might become co-heirs with him.

• In his meekness, his humility and self-determined service, Jesus loved his enemies, and returned goodness to those who treated him badly.

• He emptied himself so that we might be filled.

• He was the Lion who became the Lamb.

• Humans are born so that they may live, but Jesus, the Eternal Son of God, God in the flesh, was born to die – so that humans might be transformed and spiritually reborn, never to die.

• He came to us as a man of sorrows, acquainted with grief, for our sake. He came to serve us, rather than to be served by us.

• Far from being characteristics that are humanly produced, gained by human effort, these eight *Be-attitudes* are God's gift to us – they are his handiwork, lived in our lives through Jesus.

• These eight blessings are actually the very mind and heart of Jesus himself.

• ***These eight blessings are not rules for better living. They are not religious prescriptions*** for happy, successful Christian living.

• ***These eight blessings are gifts of God***, rather than goals God intends for us to achieve as a result of our hard work and effort.

There's an old story about a young boy from Kansas who was visiting Washington, D.C. with his family, and after the family visited the Washington Monument the little boy was so impressed that he told one of the security guards that he would like to buy it and take it home.

So the guard stooped down and looked the little boy in the eye, and said, "Well, how much money do you have?" The little boy pulled out a quarter from his pocket, and the guard said, "That's not enough."

The little boy said, "I thought you would say that, so I have some more money in my other pocket." He pulled out a dime and two pennies.

The guard stood up and said, "Son, you need to

understand three things: 1) 37 cents is not enough to buy this monument. 2) 37 million dollars would not be enough, because the Washington Monument is not for sale. 3) My third point is a question – can you tell me where you live and where you were born?"

The little boy proudly said, "I was born in Kansas and I still live there with my family."

The guard smiled at him and said, "That's my third point. You are an American citizen and the Washington Monument already belongs to you. You can't buy it because it's already been given to you."

The eight blessings of the Be-attitudes are gifts of God's amazing grace. Like the little boy learned when he tried to buy the Washington Monument, we need to realize that we can never buy or purchase these eight gifts of God's grace. If we have been spiritually transformed, if we have accepted God's grace, we have already been given these blessings. If we live in his kingdom, by his grace, these blessings are a gift. If we are the children of God by his grace, the eight Be-attitudes are our birthright blessings of God. If we are alive in Christ *we are being renewed day by day* (2 Corinthians 4:16) and we are maturing in Christ in such a way these blessings grow in our lives.

The Fourth Beatitude

Blessed are those who hunger and thirst for righteousness,
for they shall be filled.
– Matthew 5:6

If you are one of the hundreds of millions who struggle with your weight, you might have fantasized about not craving and enjoying the foods you do. Those of us who seem to always be peeking at the scale, realizing we would do well to shed a few pounds, might be tempted to think what a blessing it would be not to have an appetite.

But loss of appetite can be a serious, potentially life-threatening condition. Loss of appetite can potentially have a serious impact on our health – it's one of the conditions that a doctor's staff asks us to divulge while we're waiting to see a doctor.

Hunger and thirst are beneficial needs. We might say that hunger and thirst are blessings, natural desires God has created for us to have so that our life might be sustained.

God creates humans with a desire to know him, creating us with a spiritual deficiency. God creates us with a desire to connect with him and to be spiritually nourished by him. And as we yield to and grow in his grace and knowledge, he increases our spiritual appetite so that we *hunger and thirst* for his righteousness.

And what exactly is the righteousness of God? The foundational food in God's nutritional system is Jesus, the Bread of life. The Lord's Prayer (Matthew 6:9-15) instructs us to ask God for our daily Bread, and we can understand that instruction both physically and spiritually.

In the sixth chapter of the Gospel of John we read that Jesus is the true Bread that comes down from heaven, and Jesus, that true Bread, will enable the one who hungers and thirsts for him to eat of him and never die.

When we eat of Jesus, we find that we cannot get enough of him. When he feeds us, we always keep coming back for seconds and thirds.

After the prodigal son rejected his father and left home for a far country, he found that his choice to reject the father's love produced horrible consequences. The consequences of the prodigal son's choices meant that he was without resources to buy food and he longed to fill his stomach with anything. He was so hungry that he even desired the garbage he was feeding to pigs.

Luke 15:17 says the son came to his senses and had a change of heart, spiritually. I believe this parable tells us once the son realized he needed his father, then God opened his eyes to grace. I believe that God started to restore a spiritual appetite within his prodigal son.

The prodigal son started to long for the spiritual food he had rejected, the food his father could provide. So, hungering and thirsting for the Bread of life, the prodigal went home.

This appetite is a divine gift, a blessing of God's grace, a *Be-attitude*. Blessed (happy and contented) are they who hunger and thirst for righteousness, for they will be filled.

The Fifth Beatitude

Blessed are the merciful, for they will be shown mercy.
– Matthew 5:7

Question: If God doesn't require us to do good things *before* he blesses us, how about this verse? Many who are blinded by performance-based religion believe when Jesus says *blessed are the merciful, FOR they will be shown mercy* Jesus is explicitly teaching our "gift" of mercy is directly related to the mercy we earn by our performance.

Answer: First – a gift is not earned, it is given without qualifications or prerequisites. Second – if Jesus meant that God only gives us mercy if we are first of all merciful to others, and if Jesus meant that God will only forgive us AS or WHEN we first forgive others, then we are all in a world of hurt.

Apart from God, we have no idea how to extend divine mercy and forgiveness. Sure, we can be merciful and forgiving to some extent but Jesus was not talking about human mercy and forgiveness. Jesus was talking, both in this Beatitude about showing mercy, as well as in the Lord's Prayer about forgiveness (Matthew 6:12), about God's mercy and God's forgiveness.

How then, pray tell, can we extend and offer God's mercy and God's forgiveness if we have not first received and experienced God's mercy and forgiveness ourselves?

This misunderstanding about how we must first of all forgive and show mercy before God will extend mercy and forgiveness to us is due to the mindset that many have when reading these passages.

Many are convinced, as a result of living in the Western world, of pragmatism. Pragmatism is cause and effect. Many within Christendom believe that a right effort will bring about a right result. Many sincere church-goers believe that they can cause, by their behavior, failure or success.

Christ-less religion capitalizes on this ingrained thinking, and perverts teachings like these grace-based Beatitudes so that many believe they are some kind of litmus test for "getting saved" and "getting into" heaven. The idea is that we'll "make it" if we work hard to behave as we are told.

But Jesus was not teaching cause and effect. The new covenant, embodied within the teachings of Jesus and his disciples in the pages of the New Testament, is absolutely crystal clear:

The fact that you or I may show incredible mercy to another person will never earn our salvation.

The fact that you or I may extend mind-boggling, staggering forgiveness to someone who has harmed or injured us does not mean we deserve God's forgiveness.

If we accept this corrupted interpretation of this Beatitude, then we will think that God will not be pleased with us *until* we are merciful to others.

Christ-less religion does its best to deceive us into thinking this list of Beatitudes is nothing but a list of magic formulas, so that once we behave as Jesus tells us to, then nothing bad will ever happen to us, because we will be blessed. This corrupt religious interpretation of this grace-based teaching of Jesus says that once we work hard to do good stuff, then God will bless us and not curse us.

But that Christ-less notion falls apart in just a few verses, when Jesus says, in vs. 10, that those who accept God's grace are blessed because they are persecuted.

When we turn this corrupt religious interpretation right side up, or rather when we read how Jesus turns it right side up, then here's what we realize:

When we have received God's mercy, we are blessed by becoming conduits of his mercy. *When we accept God's remarkable mercy that we can never earn, then Jesus' mercy lives within us, and we are, by definition, merciful individuals.*

God fills us with his mercy and that fills us with deep and abiding joy – the realization that God has been merciful to us 1) fills us with joy and 2) equips us to pass on his mercy to others.

As we grow in his grace, he matures us, and because of the spiritual growth that Jesus grants us, we become more merciful. As God's dear children, we know that he does not require us to do the impossible. He does not expect us to earn his mercy by being merciful to other people.

We are blessed to be able to extend mercy to others because God has first of all extended it to us, and in Christ, extends his mercy in and through us. 1 John 4:19 explains: *We love because he first loved us.* That's a Christ-centered principle – *we extend and show mercy because he first extended and gave his mercy to us.*

An old story from the Wild West speaks of a rancher who had a huge ranch, often the target of thieves and rustlers who would steal the cattle. One day the rancher's hired hands caught a cattle thief. They caught the thief red-handed and took him to the ranch house.

Those were the days when penalties were enforced by those who had the power to do so, whether they were deputized or appointed to or not. When his hired hands hauled the thief before their boss and asked him what he wanted to do with him, he said, "String him up. Hang him. That will teach him a lesson!"

They hung that cattle thief, but the rancher was not as rough and tough as he seemed.

The rest of the day the rancher couldn't get the fact that he had taken the life of another person off his mind.

That night the rancher had a dream. In his dream he died and was standing at the Pearly Gates of Heaven. St. Peter welcomed him and took him to see God the Father, and asked the Father, "What do you want me to do with him?"

The Father said, "Forgive him. That will teach him a lesson."

The Sixth Beatitude

Blessed are the pure in heart, for they will see God.
– Matthew 5:8

First of all, again, we must combat the idea that somehow our efforts to become more pure in heart will result in God blessing us so that we will eventually be rewarded by seeing God.

It is oh-so-easy to be deceived into thinking that these eight Beatitudes are lists of things God wants us to produce in our lives. Rest in Christ and be assured that God will heal us and help us unlearn the principles of legalistic religion so that we might fully embrace the grace of God.

Has any human being, ever, become pure in heart, so that

by their efforts they spiritually cleanse and purify their heart and are consequently qualified to see God? Abraham, the father of the faithful, lied. Moses disobeyed God. David, a man after God's own heart, murdered and committed adultery. Peter, a disciple of Jesus, denied Jesus.

The Greek word for "pure" is also the root word for our English word *catharsis*. As you probably know, *catharsis* refers to an inner cleansing of the mind or emotions. The Greek word can also refer to the process used to refine metals so that pure in heart means an unmixed, unadulterated and unalloyed mind or heart.

Such purity is obviously far beyond the capacity or ability of any human being to produce, because we are flesh and blood. We are naturally filled with lust, greed, envy and vanity, and as long as we live in this mortal body of flesh, we will be afflicted with our nature.

Of course, as the New Testament explains, no matter how often we may stumble and fall, God chooses to see us as righteous and pure. *God chooses to see and acknowledge our "blessed" spiritual position in Christ, that is our union in Christ.* We are not pure in heart in the absolute sense, because as long as we live, we are filled with sin and impurity. But God chooses, by his grace, to see us as his dear children, adopted by him, and by his grace, a part of him, heirs of his kingdom.

What we are in Christ is called *a positional truth.* Our spiritual standing before God is based on our God-given position, our union with Christ. God sees us as transformed and reborn, and our standing before him is righteous because of Christ's righteousness, which God applies to us.

We are, by God's grace, pure in heart. Our purity in heart is a spiritual reality. God chooses to see us as pure in heart, even as he is actively transforming us (2 Corinthians 3). At the same time, we have that gift of God's purity in, as Paul said, jars of clay. The gift of God's purity is a treasure that lives within our mortal, sinful bodies and our bodies remain far from pure as long as we draw breath.

The fact that God chooses to accept us, see us and know us as pure in heart rather than as flawed and failed is yet another reason why the gospel is such good news! This one Beatitude, as we logically consider its implications, tells us that story of incredibly wonderful news!

Let's return briefly to the process of refining metals which the Greek for "pure" in heart implies.

Refining metals is a process. While refining a metal is not an instantaneous act, it has a beginning. In a similar way, whether we use words like redemption, salvation, justification or sanctification we are speaking of a process which God initiates, in and through us.

When God transforms us spiritually there is a beginning. It is a singular act, but there is also an an ongoing process. Both act and ongoing process are supervised and empowered by the *Divine Refiner, the Master Potter*.

Divine Refining leads us to "see God." God's grace supplies spiritual insight and vision so that we might come to see and know him. God's gift of purity in our hearts heals and refreshes our spiritual vision so that God becomes more visible and known to us.

The Seventh Beatitude

Blessed are the peacemakers,
for they will be called children of God.
– Matthew 5:9

Throughout the history of humanity, peace has always been highly prized but of course there are differing opinions as to how peace is gained and maintained.

There is no doubt that the peace that Jesus is talking about is an absence of conflict, violence, hatred and murder. There is no doubt that the gospel of Jesus Christ leads us to love our enemies, and leads to peace rather than war. However, this Beatitude is concerned with far more than simply a physical, political definition of peace.

This peace is a gift of God, not of a political or diplomatic process. This peace is the *shalom* of God, the **presence** of God rather than simply the absence of physical hostilities. Peace as simply the absence of violence and hostilities is often thought of as the peace that the threat of greater and superior violence brings about. This kind of peace is motivated by the fear of violence.

Civilizations have traditionally trusted in their weapons and their military force to grant them peace. That's the reason for the well-known name of a sidearm called the "Colt 45 Peacemaker."

The peacemaker Jesus is describing is one who is blessed by God's **presence**, and this role is so much more than arbitration or arranging compromises between two parties who disagree.

This peacemaker of the Beatitudes is a child of God in that God's presence enables them to proclaim and embody God's peace who is Jesus, the Prince of peace.

A peacemaker is not someone who has, by strength of character, obliterated all sin in his/her life so sin is *absent*. **A *peacemaker is someone in whose life God is absolutely present*.** We are children of God because God the Son came to us, becoming one of us, for our peace. When Jesus was born, a great company of angels praised God saying, as Luke 2:14 says, *Glory to God in the highest, and on earth peace to men on whom his favor rests.*

We become children of God through the work of the Holy Spirit, not our own efforts. John 1:12-13 tells us: *Yet to all who did receive him, to those who believed in his name, he gave the right to become the children of God, children born not of natural descent, nor of human decision or a husband's will, but born of God.*

All these Beatitudes are describing spiritual joy and peace, blessings given to those *on whom his favor rests* – to those who live by God's grace, who trust God and rest in him, putting aside their own vain pursuits to please God on the basis of their deeds, and fully embracing the favor and grace God alone can give.

We become peacemakers by God's grace, through the cross of Christ. As Paul tells us in Colossians 1:20, that the Father has, through Christ, reconciled *to himself all things, whether things on earth or things in heaven, by making peace through his blood, shed on the cross.*

Jesus absorbed and accepted all human violence and hatred in his body, on his cross, and transformed hatred and bitterness into reconciliation and peace. He is the Prince of peace.

We are his peacemakers as we are united in and through him, as he lives his risen life in us. He enables us to be his peacemakers, sharing his peace with the world at large. We are enabled to be peacemakers because, as Romans 5:1 explains ... *since we have been justified through faith, we have peace with God through our Lord Jesus Christ.*

The Eighth Beatitude

Blessed are those who are persecuted because of right-eousness, for theirs is the kingdom of heaven. Blessed are you when people insult you, persecute you and falsely say all kinds of evil against you because of me. Rejoice and be glad, because great is your reward in heaven, for in the same way they persecuted the prophets who were before you.

– Matthew 5:10-12

Notice that the phrase *for theirs is the kingdom of heaven* follows the first Beatitude, in verse 3, and now it follows the eighth and last Beatitude, here in vs. 10.

Poverty of spirit, the first Beatitude, and persecution, the eighth and last Beatitude, are the bookends of joy and inner happiness that a Christ-follower experiences.

This eighth Beatitude is stated differently than the others: one *blessed* statement is given in verse ten and then it's followed by another in verse 11. However, when we carefully read these three verses they all seem to offer further description and illustration of the one Beatitude given in verse 10.

Why would anyone be persecuted for *righteousness sake*? If you do good, then why would people get upset with you? Of course, the answer is found in the life of Jesus, isn't it?

Jesus said in John 3:19, *Light has come into the world, but men loved darkness instead of light because their deeds were evil.*

The very nature of the righteousness of Jesus, who is the Light of the world, provokes the evil and nefarious deeds of darkness. That happened to Jesus, when he walked this earth doing good, and it happens now as he lives within his followers.

Darkness considers light an invasion. Spiritual darkness considers light as inconveniently illuminating practices and behaviors it would rather keep hidden. As the Light of the world Jesus came to reveal, not to conceal, and the knee-jerk human response to the revelation of Jesus Christ is hostility.

We are blessed because we are persecuted for righteousness' sake. But, again, what righteousness, or more correctly, **whose** righteousness?

This righteousness is not our own. There is nothing that we can produce or contribute to God that can remotely be defined as righteous. The righteousness that this blessing is based on is the righteousness of Jesus Christ, which God the Father credits to us because of his grace.

So once again, this is not persecution that we cause or that we invite. This is persecution that is the natural reaction of a culture and society enshrouded in darkness to the Light of Christ shining in the lives of those in whom he lives.

As a further distinction and illustration of the persecution we will (as Christ-followers) experience, people will insult us and lie about us. No one enjoys being insulted. No one appreciates lies being told about them.

Jesus is not suggesting that we should take some perverted or twisted pleasure when we are persecuted. But he is suggesting that we should not be shocked when we are persecuted, because following Christ means that we will be disliked, made fun of, denied membership or employment, discriminated against, ostracized and lied about.

Jesus is simply saying the kingdoms of this world react negatively to the kingdom of heaven, so you should not be surprised when such negative and painful experiences happen, and you can count them as blessings in the sense that *they may well be proof* that Christ is living in you.

I said *"may well be proof"* because the fact that someone might insult you, persecute you and lie about you is not one and the same as proving that you are in Christ and that he is in you. It is possible (entirely possible, in fact it is probable) that human beings, of and by themselves, will cause other human beings to hate them, to insult them, to persecute them and lie about them.

For example: Pride and arrogance cause negative reactions. Sometimes church-attending people believe they are better than those who do not. They act in a haughty and superior manner towards others, they are persecuted and then, hey presto, they think that other people don't like them because they are Christians!

The only thing such behaviors prove is that when you are an obnoxious jerk towards other people many will treat you as an obnoxious jerk. Some people actually believe that they are truly Christians because of the way people treat them, when in fact all such negative reactions to them prove is that they have mistreated and abused other individuals.

The persecution that Jesus is talking about as a Beatitude, as a blessing, is the persecution that happens when Jesus himself and his righteousness that lives within us by God's grace empowers us to love others, pray for them, serve them and care for them. Then, in spite of those wonderful things that Christ accomplishes in and through us, at the end of the day, we might be insulted and persecuted and lied about.

Perhaps we shouldn't say that persecution is *proof* that a person is a Christ-follower. Persecution is not so much a proof of being a Christ-follower as it is a result of Christ living in you. We might say, for example, that law enforcement officers suffer because of the nature of their profession. Not everyone likes law enforcement officers, and not everyone appreciates them.

But suffering is not a *proof* that someone is a law enforcement officer. Many people who work in other professions suffer as well. But suffering, living a hard life, can often be the **result** of being a law enforcement officer. Some police officers are "persecuted" because they, under color of their authority and uniform, abuse those they are sworn to "protect and serve."

Another aspect of this Beatitude we should consider: Jesus is not urging us, his followers and disciples, to seek persecution or provoke it by strange and weird behavior. But he is saying that as he lives his life within the lives of those of us who receive him, others will persecute, revile and belittle us. When such a thing happens it will give us inner joy, for when it truly comes "because of righteousness" it is evidence that we are God's very own children.

When persecution for righteousness sake happens, then we may rejoice and be glad. We are revolutionaries of God's grace. C.S. Lewis compared the mission of Christians as somewhat like that of Allied soldiers in World War 2 who parachuted behind enemy lines for the good of the Allied cause.

As Christ-followers, as the children of God, we are now spiritually reborn and consequently we embody and live out the life of Christ. We are living out that life having been parachuted behind enemy lines. We are part of the invasion force of the kingdom of heaven.

Of course, Christ-followers are revolutionaries of God's grace and mean no harm. We are peace-loving. We renounce violence. We worship the Prince of peace. We, as Christ empowers us, love our enemies. Christ-followers do no harm, but at the same time we boldly stand for the values of the kingdom of heaven and we courageously follow Jesus, the King of the kingdom of heaven.

We love the Prince of peace, and we are his peace-loving activists. We obey and follow the King of the revolutionary kingdom of heaven, thus we are revolutionaries of his kingdom.

We proclaim the values of another kingdom. We do not look to the kingdoms of this world for our ultimate security, and we do not trust them implicitly. We have only one King, and his name is Jesus. We trust him, we follow him, and we rely on him for our security.

The Beatitudes in Action

One pastor I know says that one of the turning points of his own spiritual life happened when he realized that God was not expecting him to produce The Beatitudes in his life, but that the attributes of The Beatitudes were what God caused and produced in his life.

His point? The Beatitudes and blessings flow out of the life of one of the sheep of Jesus' pasture as naturally as wool grows on a sheep. Wool follows – it is consequential – to the fact of being a sheep. Sheep are sheep by God's creation – spiritual sheep are transformed from what they were into a new creation, and that includes the gift of wool-like attributes of The Beatitudes.

This pastor – let's call him John – visualized what might happen after he dies. He found himself standing before Jesus and listening to Jesus tell him what pleased him about John's life.

Jesus explained, "John, I know you never went anywhere without electronic devices that told you where you needed to go – they're really a record of your life, aren't they? Look up March 24, 2004. Tell me what you were doing on that day."

John pulled up March, 2004 and scrolled down to the 24th, and smiled, "Oh yes, that was the day I gave a sermon that many people in my church said was one of the best I have ever given."

Jesus said, "No, the sermon you gave on that day is not what I am interested in. By the way John, I never listened to your sermons anyway. And by the way, it was and is *my* church John – you served me as you served them. What really pleased me on March 24, 2004 is when you stopped for a cup of coffee on your way to church. You were standing in line waiting to place your order and you saw an older lady who seemed to be upset. You walked over and asked her if you could help her. Do you remember that John?"

John responded, "No, Lord, I don't."

Jesus looked John in the eyes and said, "Well, my life in you flowed out of you and you encouraged that lady. When you stopped to talk to her, you stopped to talk to me."

A light went on in John's mind, and he said, "OK – like

what you said in Matthew 25 – *Truly I tell you, whatever you did for one of the least of these brothers and sisters of mine, you did for me* (Matthew 25:40).

Jesus replied, "Yes, exactly right. My point in the sheep and the goats part of Matthew 25 is that my sheep consistently live out the life I live in them, so much so that they cannot remember "good deeds" they do because I always live in them and reach out to others through them. It's their way of life John. OK – take a look at another day in the past, John. Look up January 18, 2006.

Remember that day?"

John pulled up the date and said, "Lord, yes, I think I see what you are pleased about. I spent the entire day working on my book, and it was on that day that I heard from my publisher they were going to publish my book. I was really excited. Is that what pleased you on that day?"

Jesus shook his head, "No John. I never read your book you know. What I do have in mind is later in the day when you stopped by McDonalds with your kids after you picked them up after a soccer game. You were in the drive-through lane. You looked in your rear-view mirror and saw a family behind you in an old car that looked like it was on its last legs. You decided to pay for their meal, so when you paid the cashier for your meal and for your children, you told her you wanted to pay for the car behind you as well. That pleased me John. That man and his wife never really had anyone help them in any material way. You had already received your meal and you had continued on your way home when they pulled up to the cashier. When she handed them the food they ordered and told them that the car ahead of them had paid for their meal they could not believe it. When you fed them, John, you fed me."

As he told me this story, John said that it's a dream he has of the future that helps him remember that Jesus is not impressed with religious trophies and medals and ribbons. Jesus is pleased when we live our lives in such a way that we reflect his light to others. For a Christ-follower, living out the Beatitudes is as normal and natural as wool on a sheep.

Final Thoughts

Before re-reading the Beatitudes, let's remember, in summary:

1. It is a mistake to read these eight beautiful sayings as if Jesus is presenting a list of demands that he expects us to fulfill in our lives by virtue of our own efforts.

2. The Beatitudes are beautiful sayings because Jesus paints a masterpiece of what a transformed person in whom he lives his risen life will gradually begin to look like.

3. The Beatitudes are thus, as we have said before, a description of what God in Christ will produce in our lives rather than a prescription of what he expects us to accomplish – an impossible task if there ever is one!

4. The Beatitudes are beautiful sayings that describe the

gifts that we are invited to receive rather than a do-it-yourself project he expects us to build and produce.

Since beginning this project, I have been focused on the Beatitudes and the many interpretations these "Beautiful Sayings" are given. One is never finished marveling at these "Beautiful Sayings" and reluctant though I may be, knowing so much more deserves to be said, I conclude with some final thoughts. Based on the writings and teachings of many I have read even during this time of writing and editing, permit me to offer a contemporary commentary on each Beatitude.

Blessed are the poor in spirit, for theirs is the kingdom of heaven.

Blessed are those whose lives are transformed by Jesus. They recognize their moral and spiritual poverty and are saved from the affliction of self-righteousness and spiritual pride, the enemy of the love and grace of God. Blessed are those who have turned away from spiritual scorekeeping, realizing that nothing they do will ever amount to the goodness and grace of God. Their poverty of spirit reveals the lavish grace of God poured out in their lives. They are happy and contented because they do not feel superior to others, and are filled with God's goodness rather than being full of themselves.

Blessed are those who mourn, for they will be comforted.

Blessed are those who embrace Jesus and are enabled to know and reflect his sorrow for the plight of all their fellow citizens of planet earth, and for the sin-sick and corrupted good earth itself. Blessed are the heartbroken, filled with the sorrow of Jesus, weeping at funerals and beside hospital beds as terminal diseases have their way with their friends and loved ones, as Jesus himself wept. Christ-followers are at peace as they face loss – rather than hiding or being in denial of loss and grief. Christ-followers are secure in their Savior and Lord, even as they walk through the valley of the shadow of death, reflecting Jesus to others.

Blessed are the meek, for they will inherit the earth.

Blessed are those whose life in Christ is characterized by how they avoid angry, pride-filled confrontations. Happy and contented are those who have died in Christ, so that their new, spiritually resurrected person lives out the meekness and humility of Jesus. They have been given the mind of Christ, and experience true joy as they rest in him.

Blessed are those who hunger and thirst for righteousness, for they will be filled.

Blessed are those who drink deeply of Jesus, and whose spiritual hunger is filled and satisfied by the Bread of life. Blessed are they who have come to the end of themselves and their attempts to earn God's favor so that they rest securely not in capricious and preposterous attempts of works righteousness but in the righteousness of Jesus, given to them by God's grace.

Blessed are the merciful, for they will be shown mercy.

Blessed are Christ-followers who embody, by the grace of God, mercy and value forgiveness and reconciliation over retribution and vengeance. Blessed are those who have turned their backs on condemnation and instead are eager and quick to pass on the forgiveness of God.

Blessed are the pure in heart, for they will see God.

Blessed are those whose spiritual vision has been given to them by God's grace so that where others see defeat and loss, they can see beauty and potential, as they light candles rather than curse the darkness. Happy, at rest and at one in and with Jesus are those who are sincere, authentic and genuine, without lies and deception, and in so doing, give glory to God.

Blessed are the peacemakers, for they will be called children of God.

Blessed are the children of God who seek the peace of God, actively working for reconciliation rather than strife, warfare and violence. Those who stand for peace, not hatred – for healing and wholeness for all – reflect the attributes of their Lord and Savior whose risen life lives within them.

Blessed are those who are persecuted because of righteousness, for theirs is the kingdom of heaven. Blessed are you when people insult you, persecute you and say all kinds of evil against you because of me. Rejoice and be glad, because great is your reward in heaven, for in the same way, they persecuted the prophets who were before you.

Blessed are those whose Christlike motives are mis-understood and even ridiculed as they live out and experience the kingdom of God now, in the midst of darkness and evil. They are blessed and happy as they follow Christ, enduring hardships and oppression, tyranny and discrimination in his name.

Praise and Thanksgiving

Our Father in heaven,

All that we are and that we will ever be originates from you. Any virtue or goodness in our lives is ultimately a gift from you and a reflection of your glory. In and through the eternal Word, you came in the person of Jesus, revealing your love, goodness and grace. You – Father, Son and Holy Spirit – were pleased to have all divine fulness revealed in Jesus.

We give thanks for the beatific Beatitudes – the blissful and divine, beautiful sayings of Jesus. They are the mind, heart and soul of Jesus Christ, and in his humility and his self-sacrificing love we see the fulness of God. Thank you for the divine bliss of these Beatitudes imparted to us by grace, in and through the life of our risen Lord. We give thanks for our daily transformation in you so that the divine attributes of the Beatitudes grow in us as we mature in Christ and as God the Holy Spirit works in and through us.

You have blessed us with all spiritual blessings in Christ. From you, through you and because of you all blessings flow. Praise, glory and honor to Father, Son and Holy Spirit.

As it was in the beginning, is now and ever will be, forever and ever.

In the name of the Father and of the Son and of the Holy Spirit.

Amen.

Also by Greg Albrecht

Wonders of His Love

Wonders of His Grace

Letters to My Friends

A Taste of Grace

Rejecting Religion

Spiritual Soup for the Hungry Soul
(3 volumes)

Unplugging from Religion

Between Religious Rocks and Life's Hard Places

Revelation Revolution:
the Overlooked Message of the Apocalpyse

Bad News Religion:
the Virus that Attacks God's Grace

Available on www.ptm.org and Amazon